Thoughts and Things

For lovely things
   I hear and see,
And happy thoughts
   That come to me;
Thank

A mother known to the writer was asked by her small son at bedtime, "Is God nicer than you, Mummy?"

"Yes, ever so much nicer," was the answer.

"Then he must be nice," murmured the child, settling comfortably to sleep.

—From *Present Day Problems in Religious Teaching,* by Hetty Lee. The Macmillan Company, publishers.

The prayers in this book were contributed by the following:

ELIZABETH McE. SHIELDS

EDNA DEAN BAKER   JESSIE ELEANOR MOORE

Prayers of Love
and Thanksgiving

THE INCIDENT of a child's asking if God is as "nice" as his mother, quoted on the preceding page, suggests an important early step in helping children to know God. They can make a beginning in understanding the love of God through experiencing the love of parents and adult friends. Let us, then, call the attention of little children to the kind and helpful persons in their world. "See your nice clean suit! Aunt Mary washed it and ironed it for you. Aunt Mary loves you."

Or, when the child has new shoes, "Daddy gave us money to buy new shoes. Daddy loves you." Or, as the child sees a policeman directing traffic, "See, the policeman is helping us to cross the street safely. The policeman helps us."

As the understanding of love grows through

such experience, "God loves you" comes to have more meaning. Then talking with God will not be a formal matter of "saying prayers," but a happy sense of having fellowship with the Great Helper.

The mother may let the child find pictures in this book of those who have helped him. She may read one of the prayers expressing joy in the love of the family or thanksgiving for the workers of the world, as the child follows the words with the pictures. The mother may ask if he would like to say the words with her, and may read them slowly and quietly, waiting after each phrase for the child to follow.

We wish the child also to recognize directly the work of God. The little child is likely to take for granted the blessings of health, the beauties of nature, food, sleep. But, if called to his attention, they may inspire a warm sense of love and gratitude to God.

Questions about the world and delight in the fragrance, color, and motion he sees about him, often help the little child feel very close to God when he is out-of-doors. Prayers of gratitude can become very real when they grow immediately out of such experiences.

A Thank-You Prayer
for Love

We thank You, dear God,
For all who love us
And for all whom we love:

    For our fathers and mothers,
    For our brothers and sisters
    and babies,

For our teachers and friends;

We thank You, dear God,
For all who love us,
And for all whom we love.

E. D. B.

Thank God for Food

Thank You, God,
For milk and bread
And other things so good.

Thank You, God,
For those who help
To grow and cook my food.

E. McE. S.

At Our House

At our house,
Inside the door,
Are many cozy things:
The fire is warm
   and bright,
All my toys
Are ready for my play;
There's Mother dear,
And Daddy, too;
Their love and care,
Dear God,
Are just like You.

J. E. M.

In My Yard

In my yard,
Mary came to play;
She brought her
    doll and cradle,
And let me hold
Her dolly in my lap;
And Grandma gave us
Cookies for our table.
Our Father, God,
These friendly things
Make me think of You;
I thank You, God.

J. E. M.

People Who Make Me Think of God

Dear God, there are some people
Who make me think of You—
They are so kind and full of cheer,
I like to feel that they are near—
They make me think of You.

E. McE. S.

A Prayer without Words

The world is very still. dear God;
   I'd like to softly pray;
I have some lovely thoughts of You,
   But thoughts are hard to say.

Yet You can even hear my thoughts—
   The thoughts I cannot say—
And You can love a little child
   Who finds this way to pray.

E. McE. S.

Thanks for Eyes and Ears

I thank You, God, for eyes to see
A baby moon above a tree.
I thank You, God, for ears to hear
A trilling bird song, sweet and clear.

E. McE. S.

I'm Glad

I've tried, dear God,

To do my best;

I've had a happy day;

There's something sings

Inside of me,

And makes me want to pray.

E. McE. S.

Thanks for Our Bodies

We thank You, dear God,
  for our bodies:

  For we can move
    and run and jump;

  For we can speak
    and laugh and sing;

  For we can work with our hands
    to make beautiful things;

We thank You, dear God,
  for our bodies.

E. D. B.

PRAYERS

FOR LITTLE CHILDREN

And Suggestions to Fathers and Mothers
for Teaching Their Children to Pray

Abridged Edition

Edited by MARY ALICE JONES
Illustrated by SUZANNE BRUCE

AND McNALLY & COMPANY • Chicago

Thanks for Care

We thank Thee, loving Father,
  For caring through the night;
And for the joy and gladness
  That come with morning light.

E. McE. S.

An Evening Prayer

Now the sun has gone to sleep,
And birds are in their nest;
So I will thank You for my day—
My busy day of work and play—
And then I'll go to rest.

E. McE. S.

For Lovely Things

We thank You, dear God,
For all lovely things:

For the pretty flowers
And the little birds that sing;

For the butterflies,
The green grass, and the trees;

For the big shining sun,
Twinkling stars, and silver moon;

For sunset colors in the sky
And for the fleecy clouds;

We thank You, dear God,
For all these lovely things.

E. D. B.

Prayers for Help
in Being Good

THOUGH a little child is normally self-centered and we must not expect too much of him, he should begin to show love to others as well as to receive love. As soon as he does begin to think of others, he will often find that he wants to do two things at once: to do what *he* wants to do, and to do what will show love to others. And sometimes the two are in conflict. If God is real to him, he will wish to ask God to help him.

Parents and teachers will take care to avoid suggesting to the child that he pray for help in ways of behaving which contribute merely to the adult's convenience rather than to the child's development. Also, there must be some rules in the family and group which the child must obey for his safety, such as those forbidding the use of sharp knives or matches when he is alone, but about which there is no question of right or wrong. These rules should be enforced promptly and impersonally. To suggest to a child that he ask God's forgiveness for doing something in this area, or something which has merely caused his adults inconvenience, is to confuse the child, add to the weight of his adults' displeasure the awful weight of the displeasure of God, and lead the child to feel that all our impatience and misunderstanding are in the heart of God.

But the child does need help in thinking of others, and he does need to ask for forgiveness when he has knowingly done something which has hurt someone else. The prayers on the following pages suggest some of the approaches which may be helpful when used as morning prayers when the day is fresh and new, or as evening prayers when the day is over. Sometimes they may be used at the time when things have gone wrong. And it will help if the adult will let the child know that he, himself, feels the need of God's help, and sometimes asks God to forgive *him* rather than the child.

To Help Others

Help me, O God,
To use my body and mind
To find and serve
Those who need me.

Help me, O God,
To be kind and fair
To all with whom
I work and play.

Help me, O God,
To bring joy and love
And happiness
To everyone.

E. D. B.

A Prayer for Help

Dear God, I said
Some cross words
And quarreled some today,

Please help me think
Of kind words
And pleasant ways to play.

E. McE. S.

Forgive Me, God

Forgive me, God,
For things I do
That are not kind and good.

Forgive me, God,
And help me try
To do the things I should.

E. McE. S.

Like Jesus

Dear God,
I like to think
Of Jesus who was a child
Like me.

God Speaks to Me

God speaks to me
In my mind.
He speaks and says,
"Be good, be kind."